On the WING

North American Birds 1

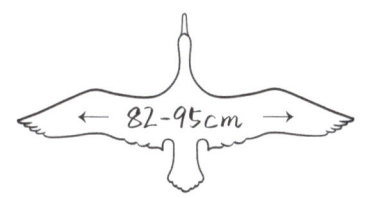

Mallard

French: Canard colvert

Super wings, super wings, flap flap flap...

Water ballerinas in the lakes and ponds are on the wing.

Mallards, Mallards, clap clap clap...

Dabble and perform water ballet on the wing.

American Crow

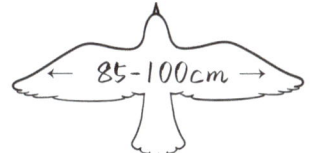

French: Corneille d'Amérique

Super wings, super wings, flap flap flap…

Black Knights in the forests are on the wing.

American Crows, American Crows, clap clap clap…

Forage for edible food on the wing.

Short-eared Owl

French: Hibou des marais

Super wings, super wings, flap flap flap...

Guardians of the grasslands are on the wing.

Short-eared Owls, Short-eared Owls, clap clap clap…

Hunt at dawn and dusk on the wing.

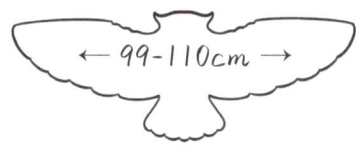

Barred Owl

French: Chouette rayée

Super wings, super wings, flap flap flap...

Rangers of the old forests are on the wing.

Barred Owls, Barred Owls, clap clap clap...

Turn their head and scan for prey on the wing.

Northern Harrier

French: Busard des marais

Super wings, super wings, flap flap flap…

Hunters on the grasslands are on the wing.

Northern Harriers, Northern Harriers, clap clap clap…

Hear and spy on prey on the wing.

Double-crested Cormorant

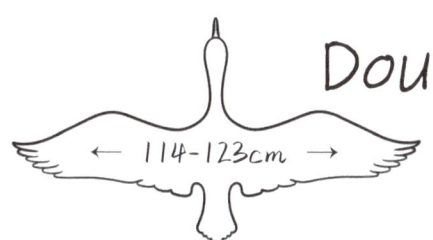

← 114-123cm →

French: Cormoran à aigrettes

Super wings, super wings, flap flap flap…

Divers in the lakes and ponds are on the wing.

Double-crested Cormorants, Double-crested Cormorants, clap clap clap…

Dive deep in one breath on the wing.

Glaucous-winged Gull

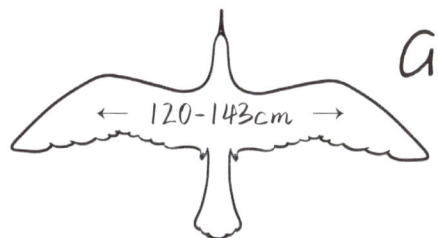

French: Goéland à ailes grises

Super wings, super wings, flap flap flap...

Guardians of the shorelines are on the wing.

Glaucous-winged Gulls, Glaucous-winged Gulls, clap clap clap...

Forage on fish and other foods on the wing.

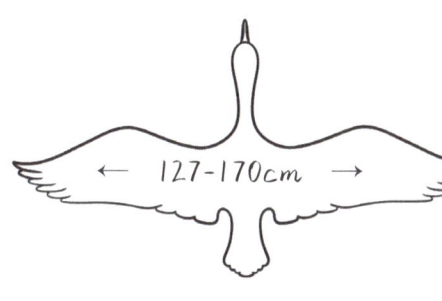

Canada Goose

French: Bernache du Canada

Super wings, super wings, flap flap flap…

Pilots in the marshes are on the wing.

Canada Geese, Canada Geese, clap clap clap…

Fly in a V-formation on the wing.

Osprey

French: Balbuzard pêcheur

Super wings, super wings, flap flap flap…

Pirates in the oceans are on the wing.

Ospreys, Ospreys, clap clap clap…

Clasp a fish and perform a "sky-dance" on the wing.

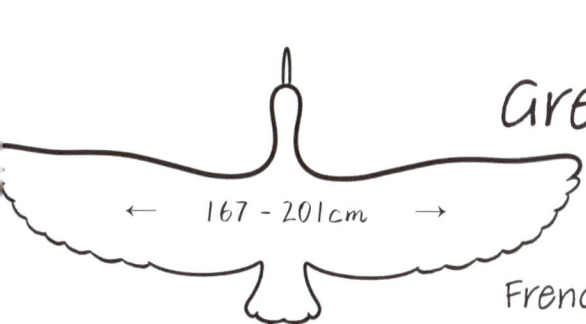

Great Blue Heron

167 – 201cm

French: Goéland à ailes grises

Mighty wings, mighty wings, flap flap flap...

Fishermen in the marshes are on the wing.

Great Blue Herons, Great Blue Herons, clap clap clap...

Stalk and gulp down fish or frogs on the wing.

Sandhill Crane

← 200cm →

French: Grue du Canada

Mighty wings, mighty wings, flap flap flap...

Ballroom dancers in the marshes are on the wing.

Sandhill Cranes, Sandhill Cranes, clap clap clap...

Perform a graceful dance on the wing.

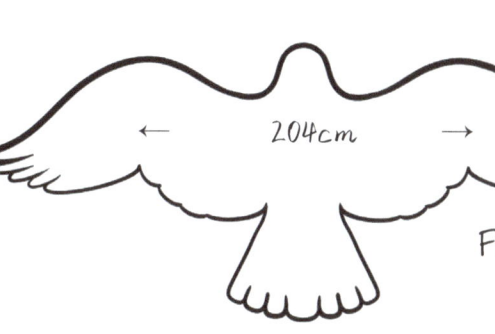

Bald Eagle

204cm

French: Pygargue à tête blanche

Mighty wings, mighty wings, flap flap flap...

Circus performers in the forests are on the wing.

Bald Eagles, Bald Eagles, clap clap clap...

Perform a cartwheel spin on the wing.

Super wings, mighty wings, flap flap flap…

Show us your talents on the wing.

Super wings, mighty wings, clap clap clap…

Our EARTH is full of life on the wing.

Author

Andrea Voon

Over the past few years, Andrea has learned and grown with her family as a full-time mother in Canada. Back in Malaysia, she was a Chinese immersion elementary school teacher. In 2021, Andrea started her journey as an author. Growing up in a multilingual environment, Andrea loves the beauty of languages on their own. She has the vision to publish picture books to support bilingual families in raising their children in English, Chinese, and Cantonese reading.

Photographer

Richard Han

Richard loves to practice patience through his lenses of the natural world. He enjoys observing the wildlife and photographing the natural lifestyles that animals live. He is excited to present the beautiful photos that he captured in dreamy tones and colors to all the birds lover.

Check out more books by Andrea Voon.

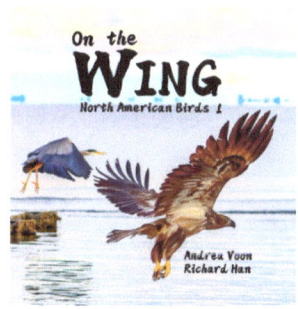
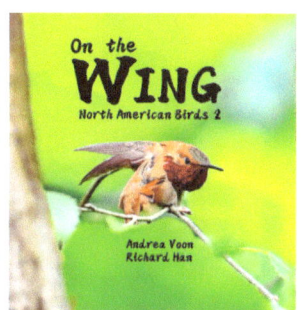
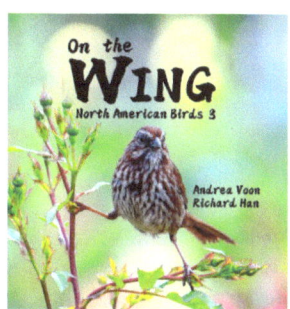
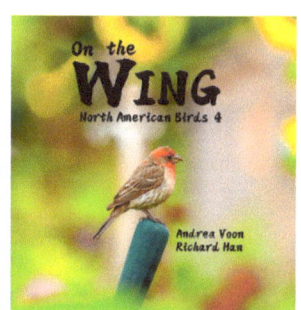

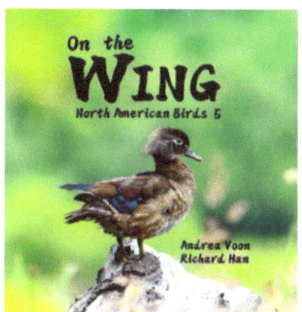

To **Shirley Han, Derek, Eliana, Alayna & Magnus Dominus**

with love -- Andrea. V

For **Richard Han**
The patience in natural photography

ISBN 978-1-998856-45-9
Text Copyright © 2024 Andrea Voon
Photo Credit © 2024 Richard Han